MW01616697

FLOW
DISCOVERY
JOURNAL

& COLORING BOOK

Daily Questions
to Spark Your Beginner's Mind

– For Children Ages 5 to 105 –

CARMEN VIKTORIA GAMPER

ILLUSTRATED BY SYBILLE KRAMER

Flow Discovery Journal and Coloring Book: Daily Questions to Spark Your Beginner's Mind – for Children Ages 5 to 105

Copyright © 2020 by Carmen Viktoria Gamper
New Learning Culture Publishing. All Rights Reserved.

Illustrations: Sybille Kramer
Back cover photo by Robert Hickling

ISBN: 978-1-7347970-5-3 (paperback)

1. Activity Book 2. Coloring Book 3. Parent Participation in Education

NEW LEARNING CULTURE PUBLISHING
San Francisco, California
www.NewLearningCulture.com

Dedicated to you

{your name here}

INTRODUCTION

Hello you!

There are 7 billion people on planet earth. You are one of them, and there is no one like you!

You have unique thoughts, opinions, likes, and dislikes, and they are important! Your mind is like a wondrous, secret world inside of you. It can create ideas no one else can. But how well do you know the secret world of your mind? In these pages, you will find questions and activities made to open your mind and learn more about yourself.

We often take our mind for granted. Instead of thinking our own thoughts, we believe what others tell us. Instead of remaining curious, we pretend to know everything. But no one ever discovered something interesting by knowing everything! The best inventions were created because someone asked a question,

and they explored their secret inner world
to find a unique answer.

The *Flow Discovery Journal* will help you be
curious and think original thoughts—the
kinds of thoughts only you can think.
By pondering the many inspiring questions,
you will get to know yourself in new ways.
There are no wrong answers. There is no way
to make a mistake. There is only exploration
and discovery!

Everyone's mind works differently.
What makes you intelligent isn't the same as
what makes someone else intelligent.
In fact, according to the developmental
psychologist Howard Gardner, there are nine
types of intelligence. For the purpose of
knowing yourself fully, three more have been
added to this book, making 12 kinds of
intelligence in total. By understanding all of
them, we can know ourselves better.
Do any of these ways of thinking
sound like you?

12 KINDS OF INTELLIGENCE

Practical Intelligence

Practical intelligence is the ability to find a solution to a problem and achieve the result you want. When you think this way, you know how to address life's big and small challenges. For instance, builders find solutions for us to live comfortably; chefs and farmers find solutions for us to eat good food. When you can fix a broken pen, repair a car, or find a way to cross a river, then you have practical intelligence.

Visionary Intelligence

Visionary intelligence is the ability to imagine, visualize, and dream of something that does not exist in the world. Inventors, explorers, and people who like to improve life use visionary intelligence. You might imagine being an amoeba and writing a story about its life, or you invent a simple microscope. By imagining, inventing, and planning, you strengthen your visionary intelligence.

Linguistic Intelligence

Linguistic intelligence enables you to understand and use spoken and written words in useful and fun ways. Writers, journalists, poets, songwriters, comedians, and teachers all use linguistic intelligence. When you express yourself through words, poetry, rhymes, songs, stories, and plays, you hone your linguistic intelligence.

Mathematical Intelligence

Mathematical intelligence is the ability to use numbers and other measurements to engage with your surroundings. Through counting, playing with numbers, solving mathematical problems, measuring things, collecting data, or identifying recurring patterns and shapes, you sharpen your mathematical intelligence.

Spatial Intelligence

Spatial intelligence is the ability to picture something in your imagination exactly as you've seen it before. You might enjoy drawing, making miniature models, or creating designs on a computer. When you remember a walk in the city, when you can rebuild a block tower the way you did the day before, or when you plan a garden, you're practicing your spatial intelligence.

Bodily-Kinesthetic Intelligence

Bodily-kinesthetic intelligence is the ability to move your body gracefully and efficiently, and to handle objects skillfully. People who love dancing, playing instruments, horseback riding, skiing, and all other sports, and hands-on activities use the intelligence of their bodies. If you enjoy moving and using your body and hands, then you exercise your bodily-kinesthetic intelligence.

Musical Intelligence

Musical intelligence is the ability to create, practice, and enjoy music, sounds, and rhythms. If you like listening to music, singing, humming melodies, whistling, or simply tapping your fingers rhythmically, you use your musical intelligence.

Empathic Intelligence

Empathic intelligence is the ability to understand, imagine, and feel what another person or an animal experiences. When you read a story and feel the character's pain and happiness, or when you pretend to be someone else when playing, you use your empathic intelligence. People with empathetic intelligence often want to help others.

Introspective Intelligence

Introspective intelligence is the ability to know yourself. It requires self-reflection, and a desire to know what you like and don't like, and why. People with introspective intelligence know that who they are isn't fixed—they are always growing, changing, and learning new things.

Naturalist Intelligence

Naturalistic intelligence is an interest in the natural world, plants, animals, and their diverse habitats. People with this intelligence track animals and identify their footprints, listen for birdsongs, camp outside, and observe insects. If you love wild animals, taking care of a pet, observing ants, naming plants on your nature walk, or growing plants, then you have naturalistic intelligence.

Existential Intelligence

Existential intelligence is the desire to ask questions about humanity: Why are we here? Where are we going? What is happiness? Why aren't more people happy? You might ask questions about the ethics of being human, or learn about different cultures or religions. Philosophers, psychologists, and everyone who likes to ponder a human's place in the universe use existential intelligence.

Intuitive Intelligence – The Flow State

Intuitive intelligence is the ability to do a task really well or know something without having to think about it. Intuitive intelligence often comes in the form of a flow state. When in flow, people don't think in words, but trust their body's intelligence and their whole being to guide their choices. Intuitive intelligence includes "Aha!" moments, and the feeling of being at the right place at the right time. When you focus on a hands-on activity, forget about time, and feel fulfilled, you are using your intuitive intelligence.

~~~~~~~~~~~~~~~~~~~~

Throughout this journal, you will discover which intelligences come easily to you, and which ones you want to practice. This is your special journey of self-discovery—use it however you want!
There are different ways you can answer the questions. For example, you can write your answer with words; if you prefer writing on lines, you can use the dots on both sides of the pages to draw lines between the points with a ruler:

.   .

.   .

Or, you can draw your answer with a pencil or colored pencils. Whether you answer one question a day or two—whether you complete this journal by yourself or with a loved one — by the end, you will feel like you know yourself better. And I hope you will know that you have something unique to offer to the world. That offering is precious and worth exploring!

Get your pencil ready, turn the page, and set out on an expedition into the secret world inside you, and the world all around!

DAY _____ 1

Imagine tomorrow is one of
the best days of your life!
What would you do?
Draw or describe it here, please:

DAY 2

What are your favorite books?

.   .

.   .

.   .

.   .

.   .

.   .

.   .

.   .

Can you imagine writing
one or more books?
What would it be about?
Draw or describe them here, please:

DAY 3

Have you ever looked through
a microscope? What did you see?
If you haven't, what do you imagine seeing?

Spark your naturalistic and visionary intelligence

Did you know that your body
is made of trillions of cells?
Imagine you could talk to all of them.
What would you say?

DAY 4

Write a letter to
yourself in the future.
Pretend you will read it
many years from now.

What would you say to
yourself? What would
you like to remember?

*Dear*_____,

DAY 5

Have you ever built something
that was taller than you? What was it?
A snowman, a blocks tower, or a building?
If you haven't, what would it be?

Spark your spatial and visionary intelligence

DAY 6

Look around the room, and outside
the window. What do you see
that would take a long time to count?
Is there anything that is completely
uncountable?

.   .

.   .

.   .

.   .

.   .

Imagine you needed exactly 36 cherries for a
special dining table decoration. What's (for
you) the fastest way or your preferred way to
count the cherries?

.   .

.   .

.   .

.   .

.   .

Spark your mathematical intelligence

How many times do you
see 4 of something
in your room,
in the kitchen,
or outside?

DAY 7

Have you ever dug your hands into dark,
soft soil? How did it feel? If you haven't,
would you like to? If not, why?

.   .
.   .
.   .
.   .
.   .
.   .
.   .
.   .

Spark your bodily-kinesthetic intelligence

Have you ever planted a seed
and watched it grow?

DAY 8

Do you know what the girl on the drawing is using? How could you find out about this?

.   .

.   .

.   .

.

Spark your practical intelligence

Can you imagine building one of these?
What would you need to build it,
and how would you do it?

.   .

.   .

.   .

.   .

.   .

.   .

What would you use it for?

.   .

.   .

.   .

.   .

.   .

.   .

.   .

.   .

DAY 9

Which items make you especially happy?
Are there certain instruments, books, toys,
flowers, foods, crystals, scents, pictures, art
supplies, clothes, or other things that lift
your spirits?

Spark your introspective intelligence

Do you sometimes have a really bad day,
when you just don't feel good?
What do you do to comfort yourself?

DAY 10

Do you know what the
object in this drawing is?
Have you ever seen one of
these outdated clocks?

Can you think of other things
that were normal many years ago,
but are rarely seen today?

Do you know someone who is much,
much older than you? Who is it,
and what do you like about them?

DAY 11

When have you last played with water?

Where were you, and how did it feel?

Could you play with water today?

.

.

.

.

.

Have you ever noticed the patterns
water makes when it flows?
How it sparkles, sprinkles,
meanders, and spirals?
You could draw some of those
patterns here:

DAY 12

Do you like when your things are in order,
with specific places for each thing?
Or do you prefer when your things
are a little messy? Why do you prefer
one over the other?

Spark your introspective intelligence

DAY 13

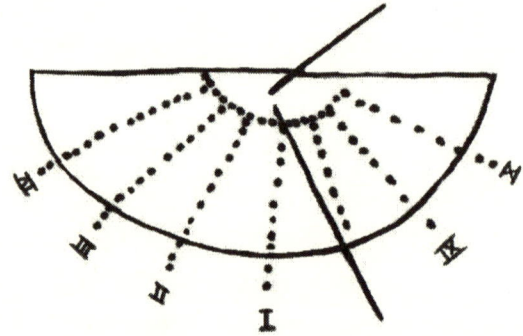

Have you ever seen a sundial?
Can you guess how it works?

.   .

.   .

.   .

.   .

Could you imagine creating one?
How would you do it?

.   .

.   .

.   .

.   .

This is a drawing of an hourglass. The sand on top takes exactly one hour to get through the narrow passage in the middle.

Can you invent another unusual way to measure time?

DAY 14 _____

Color in & add your own details to the drawing

What is your favorite meal? Draw it below,
or write down the recipe:

DAY 15

Look around your home.
Do you see something that you made
with your own hands? What is it?

What is something else you'd like
to make for your home, or to play with?

DAY 16

Have you ever been barefoot...
{color the star next to the words if your answer is yes}

☆ on the beach

☆ on moss

☆ on pebbles

☆ on dry leaves

☆ on velvet

☆ on rocks

☆ on silk

☆ in the water

☆ on grass

☆ on flower petals

☆ on metal

☆ in your socks

☆ in the mud

☆ in the snow

Where did you place your toe?

I would love to know!

DAY 17

What are your favorite flowers?
What do you feel
when you see and smell them?

.   .

.   .

.   .

.   .

.   .

.   .

.   .

.   .

.   .

Which kinds of flowers have you
smelled with your own nose?

Where would you go to
learn more about flowers?

DAY 18

Do you like adventures?
Make a list of the things or places
you would like to see, discover,
and explore:

Spark your visionary intelligence

DAY 19

Can you imagine being
as small as a butterfly?
What would you do? Where would you go?

.   .

.   .

.   .

.   .

.   .

.   .

.   .

Do you have a superpower?
Can you imagine having one?
What is it? What will you do?

DAY 20

What are your personal treasures?
Are there special places
where you put them?

.   .

.   .

.   .

.   .

.   .

.   .

.   .

.   .

.   .

.   .

.   .

.   .

.   .

.   .

.   .

.   .

Spark your introspective intelligence

DAY 21

Did you know that you can solve
multiplication problems
by counting points where lines meet?

For instance 14 x 12 =

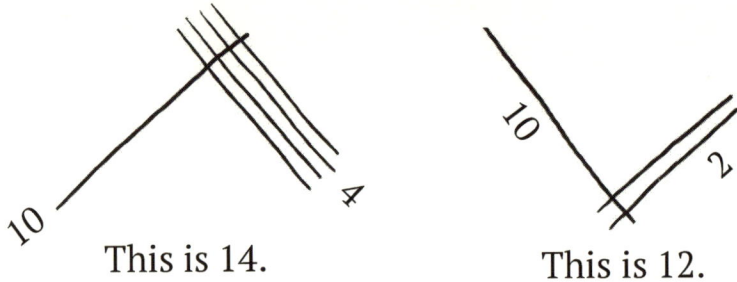

This is 14.   This is 12.

Combine the two drawings. Then,
count the intersecting points:

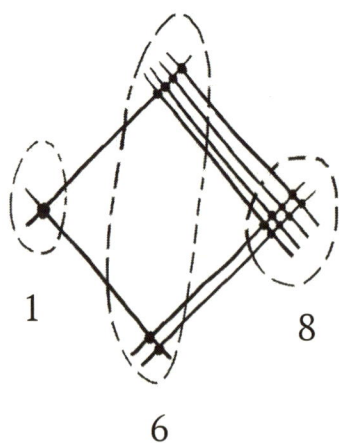

The result of this multiplication is 168.

Spark your mathematical intelligence

Now, you can try:

23 x 32 =

DAY 22

Have you ever
seen a rainbow in the sky?
Or have you seen one
somewhere else?
Can you draw a rainbow here?

Spark your naturalistic intelligence

What is your favorite
color combination? Draw a rainbow,
or anything else,
using your favorite colors:

DAY 23

How many instruments do you know?
Can you list them here?

Spark your musical intelligence

If you could play any instrument,
which one would you pick and why?

DAY 24

Have you ever crafted something fun from recycled materials, such as:

☆ an aluminum foil robot,

☆ a sock doll,

☆ a cork boat,

☆ a paper airplane,

☆ or a shoebox aquarium?

If you were to make something,
you would need materials such as paper,
tape, glue, scissors, shoeboxes, egg cartons,
aluminum foil, gift packaging material,
a needle and thread, wine corks, a sock,
buttons, plastic bottles, and bottle caps.

Spark your visionary and practical intelligence

You could create something that...

☆ moves with the wind

☆ flies in the air

☆ floats on the water

☆ makes you smile

☆ makes you laugh out loud

☆ you can give as a gift

☆ you can hang on your wall

☆ you can wear as a necklace

☆ is a game you can play

☆ makes sounds or noises

☆ doesn't make any sense at all

☆ _____

☆ _____

DAY 25

Can you imagine grownups as children?

Imagine a grownup you love
as a child.

How does that feel?

.   .

.   .

.   .

.   .

Spark your empathic intelligence

Imagine a grownup you don't like very much
as a child.
How does that feel? Do you like them more?

Have you ever asked grownups
about the games they played
when they were children?
List and describe them here:

DAY 26

Have you ever
changed your mind about something?
Maybe you tried something
you thought was scary,
and it was fun?
Or maybe you started
liking a food you used to dislike?

.   .

.   .

.   .

.   .

.   .

.   .

.   .

.   .

.   .

.   .

.   .

.   .

.

Spark your world knowledge

DAY 27 _____

Please make a list
of all the things
you love about yourself.
Please don't hold back,
but brag about yourself:

-
-
-
-
-
-
-
-
-
-
-
-
-
-
-

Please make a list
of all the things
you would like to learn,
even those you think you might
never be able to learn:

.   .

.   .

.   .

.   .

.   .

.   .

.   .

.   .

.   .

.   .

.   .

.   .

.   .

DAY 28

Did you know that cats and dogs
speak different languages?
When dogs wag their tails it means
they are happy and excited.
But when cats wag their tails
it means they are anxious and annoyed.
This might be a reason
why cats and dogs often don't get along.

Spark your empathic intelligence

Have you ever had a conflict with
someone because of a misunderstanding?
If yes, what was it? How did you discover
it was a misunderstanding?

{If not...that's amazing! I don't know anyone who had
never had a conflict because of a misunderstanding.
Congratulations!}

DAY 29

What is your favorite kind of weather,
and why?

.   .

.   .

.   .

Have you ever walked in the rain
without an umbrella? If yes, did you like it?
If no, would you like to try it?

.   .

.   .

.   .

Have you ever jumped into a puddle?
If yes, how did that feel? If no, why not?

.   .

.   .

.   .

Spark your introspective intelligence

DAY 30

Have you ever heard music
that you could feel in your body,
and you simply had to dance?

.   .

.   .

.   .

.   .

Spark your musical and kinesthetic intelligence

Listen to your favorite music
and draw it here:

DAY 31

What is something magical
that has happened in your life?

Spark your intuitive intelligence

For instance, have you ever
run into someone right when
you were thinking about them?
Have you ever unexpectedly
found something that you
needed or wished for?

DAY 32

If you could be any animal,
what animal would you like to be,
and why? Please draw or write your answer:

Pretend being that animal for a little while!
How does it feel?

Spark your empathic intelligence

What animals would
your parents or friends be?

DAY 33

Have you ever looked at the stars
for a long time? How did that feel?
What were you thinking?

.   .

.   .

.   .

.   .

.   .

Have you ever imagined infinity,
such as infinite stars, infinite sand,
infinite leaves? How did that feel?

.   .

.   .

.   .

.   .

.   .

.   .

Spark your existential intelligence

DAY 34

Have you ever invented a song,
sung a melody,
or made sounds and noises that
no one had ever heard before?
Could you do that now?

Spark your musical and visionary intelligence

Have you ever created something
that makes a fun noise,
like a sand shaker,
rice rattle,
or bucket drum?
Could you create or imagine
a new instrument right now?

DAY 35

Have you ever had
a wonderfully cozy place for yourself?
Maybe it was a fort,
or a reading corner with pillows,
or a window seat with a great view.

Describe or draw the perfect
cozy place for you:

What are some activities
that light up your spirit or relax you,
or give you an inner peace
that feels like home?
{Circle the items on the list below and add your own}

☆ Playing alone or with others

☆ Cooking a special meal

☆ Eating with family and friends

☆ Reading a book or watching a movie

☆ Painting, drawing, writing, and journaling

☆ Moving your body, dancing, or sports

☆ Experiencing nature, gardening

☆ Listening to music, singing, making music

☆ Crafting and creating objects

☆ Pondering the mysteries of the universe

☆ Having an inspiring conversation

☆ Taking a bath

☆

☆

☆

☆

DAY 36

If you could invite anyone in the world
to a tea party, who would you choose?
This guest could be a friend,
or a person who lived a long time ago,
or an imaginary person,
or a magical creature
such as a fairy godmother,
or even an animal friend.

Who would be your guest,
and what would you talk about?

Spark your visionary intelligence

DAY 37

Make a long list of things
you could do when you are bored:

· ·

· ·

· ·

· ·

· ·

· ·

· ·

· ·

· ·

· ·

· ·

· ·

· ·

· ·

· ·

· ·

· ·

· ·

Have you ever made yourself
laugh or smile?
Have you ever made someone else
laugh or smile?

DAY 38

Have you ever seen the moon
when it is full, when it is waning,
and when it is waxing?

Please draw all the different
moon shapes you have seen:

Spark your naturalistic intelligence

Isn't it interesting that the full moon
looks as if it was as big as the sun,
yet the sun is about 400 times
larger than the moon and
about 400 times farther away.

Do you think that's a coincidence,
or could this have a deeper meaning?

DAY 39

Have you ever pretended
to be someone else?
Who did you pretend to be and why?

.   .

.   .

.   .

.   .

.   .

.   .

.   .

Spark your empathic intelligence

Try it now!
How does it feel to be...

☆ a circus director

☆ a clown

☆ a lion

☆ a detective

☆ an astronaut

☆ an explorer

☆ a mother or father

☆ a ballet dancer

☆ a scientist

☆ a fireman

☆ a hairdresser

☆ a musician

☆ a prince or princess

☆ a robber

☆ an angel

☆ a teacher

☆ a police man

☆

DAY 40 _____

Some people remember being a baby.
What is your earliest memory?

.   .

.   .

.   .

.   .

.   .

.   .

.   .

.   .

.   .

Spark your introspective intelligence

What is something you wished
you remembered about being a baby?

DAY 41

Do you prefer this, that, or both...?
{Color the stars next to the words if your answer is yes}

☆ to be on stage ········ OR ········ ☆ to be in the audience

☆ to write ············ OR ················ ☆ to draw and color

☆ to sing ················· OR ····················· ☆ to dance

☆ walk ················· OR ···················· ☆ run

☆ jump ·················· OR ···················· ☆ crawl

☆ watch ·················· OR ···················· ☆ listen

☆ bike ··················· OR ···················· ☆ drive

☆ indoors ···················· OR ···················· ☆ outdoors

☆ talk ···················· OR ···················· ☆ listen

☆ loud ···················· OR ···················· ☆ quiet

☆ sweet ················ OR ···················· ☆ salty

☆ cats ···················· OR ···················· ☆ dogs

☆ apples ·················· OR ···················· ☆ oranges

☆ getting up early ············· OR ············· ☆ sleeping in

☆ only a few people ············· OR ············· ☆ many people together

Spark your empathic intelligence

DAY 42

Have you ever heard of Braille language?
People who know Braille read by moving their
fingertips across patterns of raised dots on a
page, instead of using their eyes.

Some games to play:

Prepare different kinds of foods,
such as strawberries, carrots, bananas, and
nuts. Blindfold yourself and try to figure out
which is which only by tasting them.

Prepare a bag with a variety of little items
such as a toy car, a pencil, a spoon, an eraser,
and other small things you find,
then blindfold yourself and guess which is
which by using your fingers.

Find a friend to play this game:
Draw a word on their back using your finger,
and have them guess what you wrote.

DAY 43

Do you know what this drawing is?
Many of our clothes and fabrics are made
with a bigger,
more complicated version of this.

Have you ever seen or worked
with a hand weaving loom?

Spark your world knowledge

Try crafting a simple loom.
You will need yarn
and a piece of cardboard
that is about the size
you want for your fabric.
Did you try? How did it go?

DAY 44

How do you feel
when you do something well?
Make a list of all the things
you can do well:

Spark your introspective intelligence

DAY 45

Have you ever played pretend
sword fighting? If yes, did you enjoy it?
If no, would you like to try it? Or, do you
prefer not to try it?

Spark your bodily-kinesthetic intelligence

Do you think boys/men and girls/women
are very different?
How are they different?

.   .

.   .

.   .

.   .

.   .

What things do boys/men and girls/women
have in common?

.   .

.   .

.   .

.   .

.   .

.   .

.   .

DAY 46

Are there some thing you
weren't able to do last year
but you can do them this year?
Why can you do them now?
Write or draw your list:

Spark your growth mindset

DAY 47 _____

Have you ever created a puzzle,
or could you imagine creating one?

.   .

.   .

.   .

.   .

.   .

Here is how you can create
a jigsaw puzzle: Draw a picture,
or find a photo,
and cut it in manageable pieces.
Then put it back together.

Spark your practical intelligence

Here is how you can create
a word-find puzzle:
In the space below,
write words horizontally, vertically, and
diagonally, and fill the empty spaces in with
random letters. Now find the words!

DAY 48

Have you ever wished you
could fly like a bird?
Where would you go? What would you
discover? How would you feel?

Spark your visionary intelligence

Did you know,
you don't have to believe
all of your thoughts?
If you think something you don't like,
you can ask yourself,
how else could I think about this?

DAY 49

Let's do some drawing exercises!

1. Try to draw a perfect circle:

2. Now try to draw a perfect circle
   with the hand you don't usually use:

3. Try to draw two circles using
   your right and left hand at the same time:

Spark your practical intelligence

How many different images
can be made with a circle?
Draw as many as you can!
Here are two examples:

DAY 50

This is not a fox:

It is only a drawing of a fox.

The word "f o x" is not a fox.
It is only a word that describes a fox.

Spark your existential intelligence

What is a fox?

DAY 51

Let's play with language!
Write down as many words as you
can think of that rhyme with "time."

-
-
-
-
-
-
-

Write down as many words as you
can think of that make you happy:

-
-
-
-
-
-

Now, try to write a poem that rhymes with
the words you just collected,
something like this:

I have a great time
eating ice cream
in the sunshine.

DAY 52

What would you do if you were
president and could make
new rules for the world?

Spark your empathic and visionary intelligence

What would you do,
if people asked you to
redesign the school system?
Imagine the school that
you would like to go to:

DAY 53

Have you ever seen shapes in the clouds,
like an animal, spaceship, or something else?
If yes, which ones do you remember?
If not, please go watch the clouds as soon as
you can, and describe or draw them here:

Spark your visionary intelligence

DAY 54

What makes a good friend?

. . . .

Spark your empathic intelligence

Do you think you are a good friend?
If yes, why? If no, why?

Can you imagine being
a great friend to yourself?
What would you say to yourself?
What would you do for fun?

DAY 55

This is a drawing of
a compass.
The needle always
points to the
magnetic North
pole of the earth.

Explorers use compasses to determine
their direction.

Would you be interested
in learning how to use a compass?
How could you go about that?

.   .

.   .

.   .

.   .

.   .

.   .

.   .

.   .

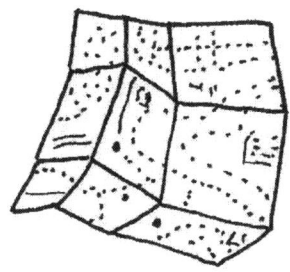 This is a drawing of a
treasure map.
You could hide a treasure
in your home, and draw a
map of where to find it.
You could give the map to a friend, and
practice using a compass to find it.
Here you can practice drawing your map:

DAY 56

If you were a tree, what kind of tree would you like to be? Please draw or write it here:

Spark your world introspective intelligence

Let's play pretend:
Stand up,
close your eyes,
and imagine for a moment
being that tree.
Feel your roots, feel your branches.
Is there wind, rain, sunshine?
How does it feel?

This is a drawing of the tree
that I would like to be.

DAY 57

Look around your room and choose
a few objects. Do you know what
they are made of?
Do you know where they came from?
How would you find out?

Spark your world knowledge

Please list some of your things here,
and tell me what they are made of
and where they came from:

DAY 58

What is your favorite
wild animal, and why?

· · ·
· · ·
· · ·
· · ·

What do you know about this
animal?
Where does it live? What does it eat?
What are the special things about
this animal?

· · ·
· · ·
· · ·
· · ·

· · ·
· · ·
· · ·

Spark your world knowledge

Imagine you could communicate
with that animal.
What would you talk about?
What would you do together?

DAY 59

Have you ever seen or walked a labyrinth?
Ancient wisdom says
labyrinths can help you find
your inner center.
Here is a special labyrinth.
Trace the black line with your finger
or with a pen, and after many rounds you will
arrive at the flower in the middle:

Here is how you can make
a simple labyrinth. You can draw it
or lay it out on the table with toothpicks
or on the ground with pebbles.
Can you find ways to make it bigger?
It doesn't have to be perfect to work.

1.

2.

3.

4.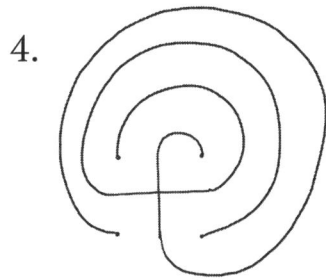

DAY 60

Thank you for playing!
Here are the last questions:

Which questions did you like the most?

.   .

.   .

.   .

Which questions will you probably
never forget?

.   .

.   .

.   .

Which questions have you
or will you ask your friends?

.   .

.   .

.   .

How about we celebrate now?
Let's be merry!
How would you like to celebrate?
{Please color the stars next to your yes .answers}

☆ dance party

☆ singing

☆ tea party

☆ lighting a candle

☆ hugging yourself or someone else

☆ getting flowers for yourself

☆ eating a special food

☆ inviting a friend over

☆ laughing out loud

☆ doing a happy dance

☆ going for a walk in nature

☆ _____

☆ _____

ABOUT THE AUTHOR

"LEARNING AND FEELING CANNOT BE SEPARATED."

Carmen Gamper

CARMEN VIKTORIA GAMPER is the author of *Flow To Learn: A 52 Week Parent's Guide to Recognize and Support Your Child's Flow State.*

Carmen is an educator, advisor, coach, and speaker for child-centered education. She became an expert on childhood flow states by supporting and witnessing hundreds of children learning on their own terms in carefully prepared, hands-on learning environments.

As founder of the New Learning Culture (NLC) program, she supports directors and staff of preschools and grade schools, parents and homeschooling families in safely offering child-directed, flow-rich learning environments.

Carmen created the *Flow Discovery Journal* to help children get away from screens, explore their own world, and eventually drop into the flow state of deep fulfilled focus –the optimal state for learning. The book is designed to be interesting for grown-up children, too!

Check out Carmen's website for more:
https://flowtolearn.com

ABOUT THE ILLUSTRATOR

SYBILLE KRAMER is the creator of the delightful drawings in Carmen's books. She is an artist and teacher from Alto Adige/ South Tyrol, Italy. She is married and has two grown up sons and two dogs.

Sybille discovered her love for hands-on learning when her children went to a Rebeca Wild based, Montessori-inspired elementary school, and afterwards, when she homeschooled them through middle school.

Sybille turned her passion for hands-on learning into her profession and has since supported teachers and parents with the learning materials and classes she developed. She is one of driving forces of Homeschooling Italia, and also supports teachers in public schools.

Currently, Sybille is developing an online class together with Carmen to offer her delightful hands-on learning materials for preschool and grade school-aged children.

Check out her blog:
https://sybilletezzelekramer.wordpress.com/

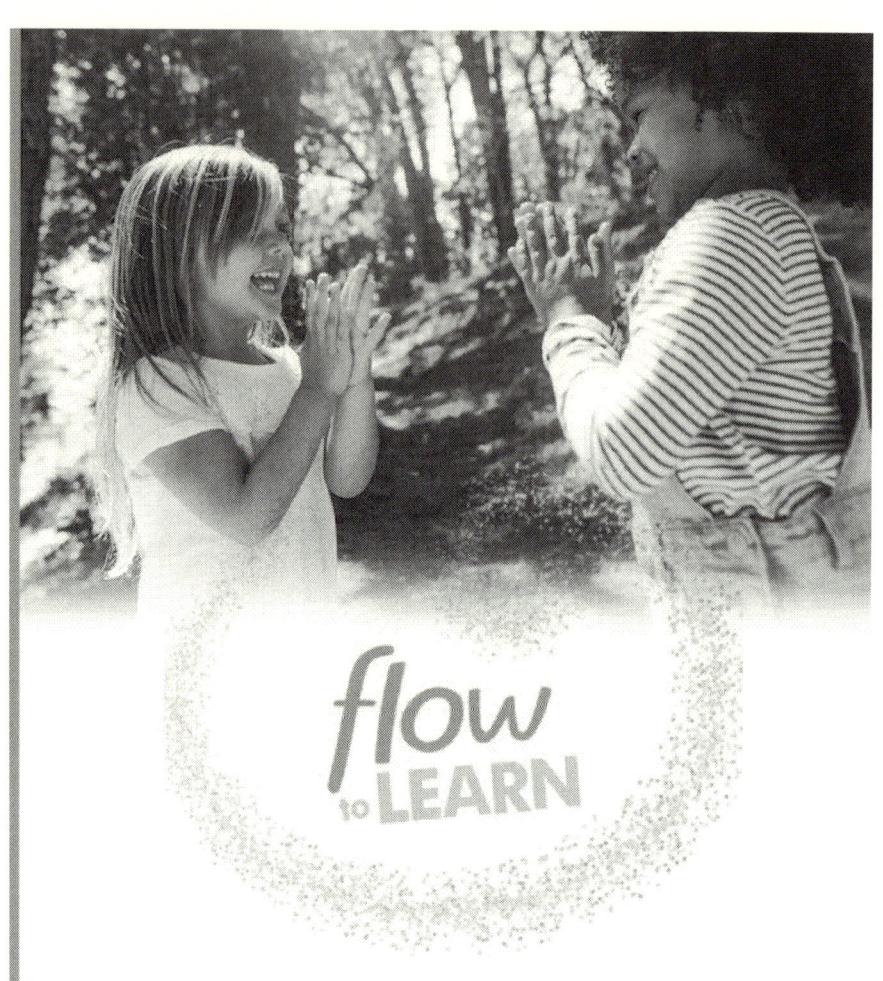

flow to LEARN

A Parent's Guide to Recognize and Support
Your Child's Flow State - the Optimal
Condition for Learning

Carmen Viktoria Gamper

THE PARENT's GUIDE: *FLOW TO LEARN*

*Flow To Learn: A 52-Week Parent's Guide
to Recognize and Support Your Child's Flow State
– the Optimal Condition for Learning*

FLOW TO LEARN is an uplifting, illustrated parent's guide, available in print and eBook, offering 52 weeks filled with practical suggestions and compassionate insights for creating independent play and learning opportunities for children.

Using practical, evidence-based tools from the fields of child development, psychology, and child-centered education, readers are guided step-by-step through the creation of simple hands-on activity stations that boost children's love for learning.

In these prepared environments, children naturally experience flow, the deeply focused state scientifically proven to be the optimal condition for learning.

Explore the 52 inspiring chapters to enrich every week of the year:

☆ Create activity stations in your home to free up your time while strengthening your child's intelligence and mental health
☆ Discover your child's vibrant inner world, and support them through the ups and downs of childhood
☆ See children as guides to your own flow state to bring more fun, meaning, and purpose into your lives

Each of the 52 Weeks of Flow To Learn offers two parts: First, readers find reflections and information about flow, then an array of practical suggestions, "Try This," on how to facilitate flow in life with children.

Some Weeks offer authentic and encouraging insights from an experienced mother who incorporates the flow-parenting approach with her family.

Throughout the book, you will be delighted by the many illustrations of children and adults learning in flow.

YOU CAN PURCHASE FLOW TO LEARN
ON AMAZON, BARNES & NOBLE, and INGRAMS.

Made in the USA
Middletown, DE
29 January 2021